praying by heart

praying by heart

Prayers

for

Personal

Devotion

and

Public

Worship

KAY BESSLER NORTHCUTT

UNITED CHURCH PRESS
Cleveland, Ohio

For my mother and father, Thelma and Clint Northcutt,
and my sisters, Nancy and Amy,
who provided me the gift of love

For my husband, Joseph,
who consummated it

For South Hills Christian Church (Disciples of Christ),
the crucible that refined it

United Church Press, Cleveland, Ohio 44115
© 1998 by Kay Bessler Northcutt

Published 1998. All rights reserved

Printed in the United States of America on acid-free paper
03 02 01 00 99 98   5 4 3 2 1

Library of Congress Cataloging-in-Publication Data

Northcutt, Kay Bessler, 1957–
    Praying by heart : prayers for personal devotion and public worship /
    Kay Bessler Northcutt.
        p.   cm.
    Includes index.
    ISBN 0-8298-1285-7 (pbk. : alk. paper)
    1. Devotional calendars.   2. Prayers.   I. Title.
BV4812.N67   1998
242'.8—dc21   98-35075
                                                                  CIP

contents

LENT

EASTER AND EASTERTIDE

ORDINARY TIME

foreword

An art form that rarely is treated artfully is the pastoral prayer as voiced in Christian public worship. This book deserves an encouraging foreword for its art.

But wait: *should* there be art in prayers designed for the weekly use of God's people? Debates, ancient and modern, pose art versus artlessness, formality versus informality, anticipation versus spontaneity in prayer.

Who can begrudge the congregation gathered to celebrate the survival of a threatened individual its moment of heart-deep artlessness? A high-school student suffers a tragic end, and an ad hoc assembly grieves: is there not place for informal tearful eruptions of voice at such a time? Sudden good or bad news reaches the people; no one could have anticipated or planned for it. Is not spontaneity in prayer then in order? Of course and of course and of course.

Such situations, however, do not represent the only way to conceive the act of praying when the people gather. Those who are suspicious of the planned, edited, and printed prayer often cite biblical injunctions that promote simple voicings of prayer. They conveniently overlook the cadenced and poetic language of those psalms that were clearly designed for use by the Qahal Yahweh, the congregation of Yahweh in Israel. Because they come in rhythmic patterns, with accents that take fresh life in translations from the Hebrew to almost anything else, these psalms become and remain memorable. We want Psalm 23 in times when confidence eludes us, or Psalm 90 when we want to be realistic hopers at graveside. We look forward to life in God's house the way the psalmist did in Psalm 27. We do so because he voiced our heart's impulses so well.

So Pastor Kay Bessler Northcutt lets us overhear a year's worth of structured utterances. These verbalizations never let their printed character and the appearance of formality distance the pray-er and the prayer from the hearts of the people who deserve the profoundest cries and the most serene words of thanks after the passage of a week and before arrival of the next seven days.

The format of such prayers puts some people off. These short lines: are they to suggest that they are poems in lazy free verse, rambles that leave a great deal of white space on the page? Reread them, and you will find instead what drew me (and my spouse) to them when we read some in manuscript: the lines tend to follow the patterns of breath—short, given the excited pulse of public worship—and the gasps of occupied minds, which we are able to keep focused at such times.

As for content: theologian William May describes the intercessory praying of a congregation as among the most public acts that occur when the doors of the sanctuary shut, to keep the people of God alone together for an hour each week. Such prayers have certain components: no element of the congregation members' lives is too insignificant to be remembered, to serve as a prompt for the prayer of all. Moving beyond that circle, there is in such prayers the impulse to include the otherwise overlooked: the homeless, the poor, the disappointed, the despairing. They make regular appearances here. Intercessory prayers are "loving the neighbor on one's knees," and love should issue from their use.

Finally, in the prayer, one remembers the enemy. Northcutt's prayers do not show a vivid sense of enemies, but implicitly "the other" comes on stage as a shadowy presence, the foe of the good.

The fact that the prayers are published keeps them from being frantically current. Sometimes pastors use the moments of prayer as a verbal bulletin board. I know a good-natured pastor who, at a White House breakfast, mentioned that others at the table—evangelists, journalists, denominational leaders, and the like—had access to mass audiences and mass media, where their moonlighting at a Washington breakfast would be covered. How could the Rev. Mr. Modest let his congregation humbly know that he was going to travel to Pennsylvania Avenue? With a sly and knowing wink, he told us that he had informed his congregation by informing God: "O God, thou knowest that this Wednesday at 8:30 A.M. I shall be conversing with the President, and, O God, thou knowest . . ."

Northcutt is not for using the pastoral prayer as such a bulletin board. Yet despite the necessary absence of headline items of current events, there is a currency to these intercessions that will remain fresh for some years to come. While Kay is a sensitive pastor who listens well and can thus speak out of and for the hearts of vulnerable people, these are not sentimental or jargon-ridden "care-and-share" outpourings. They aim to be directly about their business: of carrying on the conversation between a self-disclosing God and the people collected. The agent will be the pastor who prays off these pages, using words by an expressive author who has the grace to move herself offstage and let the prayers be those of "we" and not of "me." Let us pray.

Martin E. Marty
The University of Chicago
The Public Religion Project

acknowledgments

As a young associate pastor, I was called to a church that knew how to pray together. Each Sunday morning as they bowed their heads and drank in the silence, they became the body of Christ, whole and pulsing with life. I am indebted to South Hills Christian Church (Disciples of Christ) for their formation of me through the work of prayer and to Bryan Feille, my senior pastor, who graciously gave me the responsibility and privilege of each Sunday's pastoral prayer.

Saturday nights, prayer-writing nights, were my favorite of the week. In our tiny apartment, I pored over the Psalms, with John Rutter's "Gloria and Other Anthems" playing at full tilt. Sometimes, a few hours into the process, when the right phrase eluded me, my husband Joseph would insert himself at the computer keyboard and write something to get me off high center. His words comprise some of my favorite images in this little book, including "build in us a house of rest."

From the moment that pastoral praying became my work, I began to adhere myself to the words and work of Madeleine L'Engle, Ruth Duck, Brian Wren, and Ann Weems. They have had a profound influence on my spiritual development. This little book is indebted to them and contains allusions to their words and phrases.

My friend Stephanie Paulsell, a young pastor responsible for prayer in her church of Rockefeller Chapel, mailed her bidding prayers to me weekly. Her uncommonly beautiful words and images, combined with her exquisite spirit, breathed life into my own prayers.

My pastor during my growing-up years, Jerry Johnson of Western Oaks Christian Church (Disciples of Christ), was the most formative voice shaping my prayer. He brought a candor and tenderness to prayers that astonished me even as an adolescent. Jerry taught by example that laughter and lament both belong in prayer, along with everything in between. Everything belongs to the words and work of prayer.

Bert Cartwright, pastor, mentor, and friend both to me and to South Hills Christian Church, deserves credit for this little book. Bert insisted that I collect my pastoral prayers for a book. When I did not, he secured copies of my prayers, then organized, titled, and collated them in book form. Bert brought order out of chaos. I regret that these prayers were not published before his death.

Ambrose Edens lovingly tormented me each Sunday morning, "clocking" my prayers. As I bowed my head, in the last instant before closing my eyes to pray, I would glimpse Ambrose as he punched the second-hand timer of his watch. His favorite prayers inevitably clocked in at ninety seconds. Ambrose taught me the pragmatics of the pastoral prayer: not too long, not too fast.

It was my very good fortune to have Martin Marty as my teacher. He read my prayers during Advent one year, adding his and Harriet's responses. I am deeply grateful for Marty's labors over my prayers. Without his attentiveness and encouragement these prayers would have remained in my file cabinet, yellowing at the corners.

Penny Fruth and Stephanie Paulsell, two of my favorite writers, read, reread, and edited these prayers. They lovingly trimmed what needed pruning but, more important, never flagged in their encouragement. Nancy Ray, one of those devoted and fervent-praying elders of Harvard Avenue Christian Church (Disciples of Christ), prayed for the completion of this book as part of her daily prayer discipline. She, along with Barbara Jones and Christine Kessler Chenoweth, persistently inquired about its progress. I am grateful for such friends.

My brilliant younger sister, Amy Northcutt, edits every word I write. With a mind like a razor and a kind heart that understands me well, Amy provides invaluable guidance.

The Tuesday morning prayer group of First Christian Church (Disciples of Christ) in Sand Springs, Oklahoma, prayed me through the final push of this project. My thanks go to Dorothy Spence, Doris Benton, Marie Weaver, Dorotha Randall, Bobbie Dillahunty, Rosa Lee Clem, Vera Nell Boatman, Gerry Wolf, Barbara Fisher, Norma Jones, Thelma Bradshaw, and Anne and Ray Fritts.

Finally, I am grateful for the generosity of my benefactors for providing writing tools and time and for graciously sharing both wisdom and resources as I need them.

❧ *Advent*

O GOD OF STEADFAST LOVE!
First Sunday of Advent

O God of steadfast love,
of unending mercies to us,
new every morning

You gave us this garden earth
and unequaled gifts of the sun,
the rainbow,
the breath of life.
You parted the Red Sea and sent manna
and prophets.
You gave us children and one another.
Accept our longing of joy and hope
for the promise
of yet one more gift,
our Messiah, the Christ,
your Child

We wait
with Elizabeth, barren and advanced in years,
and with Mary, surprised by Gabriel's announcement.
We wait
full of hope in the face of hatred and warring,
knowing there is no hurt deep enough,
no disaster shattering enough,
knowing there is no Herod strong enough
to stop this promise
of the babe, the child of Mary

For someone on earth will see the star;
someone will hear the angel voices;
someone will run to Bethlehem;
someone will know peace and goodwill.
The Christ will be born

Accept our prayers for healing
in this time of increased loneliness.
Even as we wait and hope for the coming of your Child,
we miss absent friends and loved ones

Come, long-expected Christ child,
whose first, miraculous, newborn cries
fill our hearts again
with hope, with joy.
O come, Emmanuel! Come

AMEN

❈   ❈   ❈   ❈

HOPE, FULL-BLOSSOMED
AND BRIGHT
Second Sunday of Advent

God of creation and love,
on this second Sunday in Advent
we feel hope, full-blossomed and bright,
taking root in our souls again.
And it is difficult to confess it,
even to you, Lover of our souls,
because so much we have hoped for in the past

has failed fulfillment;
so much of what we hoped for
has left us vulnerable and hurt;
so much of what we have hoped for
has misled us, misdirected our lives

Vulnerable and uneasy,
we come praying for a heart full of wisdom this Advent
that we might discern
what is worth hoping for.
For surely hope is born
when this child of Mary's takes a first, gasping breath

How we wonder that you, Creator of light and life
and spinning comets,
expressed yourself to us in an infant,
an infant whose cries
give voice to
our own laments of anguish
over our fragmented lives,
broken through what we have done
and what we have failed to do.
Knit our torn pieces into a new garment
until our whole lives sing out
the clarity of love

We remember and call to you on this holy day
unseen workers,
those who lift and clean and nurture
the bodies and the minds and the spirits
of those we love who are in nursing homes
and receiving hospice care

We cry out for peace, God,
while the seduction of power and resources and greed
frantically tries to keep the world and our leaders
closed to one another

May the God of Sarah and Abraham
and Mary and Joseph
hear our prayers

AMEN

❧　❧　❧　❧

BURN IN US, GOD
Third Sunday of Advent

O God!
You led your people
through the wilderness
with a pillar of fire by night.
Burn now in our hearts
as we wait for the light:
your promised Child

For still, God, we wander in a wilderness
that threatens to consume us.
We give in to the pressures of our culture,
rushing to meet expectations we cannot fulfill.
We diminish the glory of this life you gave us,
living it by lists of "things to do today"

Burn in us, God,
until we are like the bush Moses met in the desert:
burning but not consumed

Hear our prayers of confession, Holy One,
that even as we are fully aware of the joy
and comfort of those we love—
in this Advent time especially—
we miss the ones who are gone from us,
separated from us by time, space, or
human misunderstanding

This season of light reminds us of the light that
has gone out of our lives—
whether sister, brother, mother, father, grandparents,
husband, wife, partner.
We miss them.
We miss those in this church community
gone before us,
now in the cloud of witness among us

Hear our prayers of gratefulness
for those we love
whose hearts are now with you.
We silently call their names to you now:

Silent prayer

Because you have promised, God,
we ask that those who grieve know comfort,
that those who know the anguish of illness receive healing,
and that those who know the heartache of estrangement
come home to the peace of restored relationship

Scrape the scales from our eyes,
that this Advent we may recognize your Child's presence
in the poor, the outcast, the addicted, the suffering
that we might be eager to find Jesus there

AMEN

✽   ✽   ✽   ✽

FULL OF DESIRE AND LONGING
Fourth Sunday of Advent

O Holy One, you struck the rock in the desert
and brought forth streams of water.
We come before you
an Advent people,
full of desire and longing
for the One who has been promised

We come this morning
longing for the desert of wilderness
we know in this world and in our lives
to be transformed into pools of water

We come longing for peace in a miraculous time
of increasing signs and wonders of peace.
We come asking again for your strength and wisdom;
for as we have cried to you for peace,
we beseech you now:
guide us in our work of nurturing and supporting
the new democratic peoples in their infancy throughout
this world

As we make this Advent journey
we confess some of our longing is born of envy.
We envy the obviously bright, obviously compelling star
the Magi and the shepherds followed

Even as we claim outward signs of hope
and gratefully prepare for Christ's advent,
some of us struggle inwardly with Gethsemanes of
betrayal, loneliness, and
brokenness in our relationships with family,
neighbor, and community

Clothe us in compassion, that we might forgive ourselves
and others as you have forgiven us,
restoring relationship, repairing

As we pray for the hungry, the ill, the grieving,
we ask for strength to respond to them and their needs
with bread, not stone

We wait, O generous God,
we wait anxiously
to cradle the babe, the child of Mary

O come, Emmanuel, come

    AMEN

    ❊   ❊   ❊   ❊

❧ Christmas
and Christmastide

GIFT-GIVING GOD
Christmas Eve

Gift-giving God,
we come to this night of mystery and birth,
our hearts over-full with
inexpressible gratitude

We have gathered here to bear witness to
love so amazing, so divine,
that nothing in our lives
is able to remain the same

For this is the night
all things
are made
new

We long, God, to cling to you so wholly
and hungrily that
we will conquer the frailty in us
which chooses self over neighbor

We listen to stories of terrified shepherds
prostrate before the songs of angels.
And we find ourselves wanting and dreading
that same kind of transforming terror
for our lives

We long to love you, God,
until the gifts you have given us—
food, clothing, shelter, and our talents, too—
become in our hands as the sustaining rain in your hands:

gently falling on everyone, the earth, all creation,
water of life for all peoples

For as Christ's birth was marked by receiving
strangers' visits and gifts from the wise ones,
we will continue
to celebrate his birth
through bringing gifts
and welcoming the stranger

On this Christmas Eve,
more than any other desire,
we urgently thirst
to be your people,
recognized as the body of Christ,
devoted to Emmanuel, God–with–us,
heads bowed before the babe, the child of Mary.
Let it be, God. Let it be

AMEN

❄ ❄ ❄ ❄

AND SO IT IS CHRISTMAS
First Sunday after Christmas

And so it is Christmas, God,
the presents opened, the guests arrived,
the incarnation gently bumping into us
all around and in between and behind and before us

It is now, God,
that we discover the fruit born of our
Advent waiting-time and preparation

Perhaps
on this first Sunday after Christmas
some of us must confess
that nothing measurable has been received,
given,
or transformed for us
in the miracle birth of God-with-us, Emmanuel

It is now,
after the breathless party-whirl and
feasting have subsided,
now, in the Christmastide, that we come to discern
whether, like the stingy innkeeper,
we have managed to resist the Christ child;
or,
like those hard-working shepherds,
we are amazed dazzled and transformed;
or,
like Mary, we are consumed with pondering and praying,
overwhelmed by the change this infant has brought to our
lives

As we catch our breath in this time
of calm before the spin of New Year activities,
we long to get back to normal,
to remembering
and living
in gratitude for the gifts,
the daily gifts,
of life and breath and loving relationships

Continue, God, to lead us beside the still waters
as we resist the consuming patterns of our culture—
all these sales

that tempt us to believe
one more time
that something outside of ourselves
can fill our desire.
O, God, persist with us until
we understand that something "50 percent off" is no
bargain,
and that we will surely
miss this gift called "life"
if we do not become finally
as the lilies of the field

Hear our prayers
for those in our church who know the anguish
of illness
or of diminishment for any reason, by any cause.
As we labor over soups and letters and acts of kindness,
bless our work,
so that miraculous comfort—your comfort—
will arrive with our broth,
our words,
our work

Thank you, God, for your gift, Emmanuel.
We long,
we hope,
we pray
to fully receive it

AMEN

❋ ❋ ❋ ❋

A TWO-WEEK-OLD, WRINKLY BABY
Second Sunday after Christmas

God, we are still trying to grasp
the unimaginable mystery
of your Child in flesh appearing
and growing,
now a two-week-old, wrinkly baby
in Mary's cherishing arms

As Christmas lights are taken down and Christmas carols
are put away until next year,
we are left with
an infant who softens our hardened hearts
with lamblike, piercing cries

It is good to stay here a while
with this baby and his mother.
As the milk of life flows from
Mary,
we open ourselves to the feast of
this Child's life unfolding before us.
Surely, God,
we are not worthy to receive him.
But only speak the word, and we
shall be healed

We beseech you, God,
raise up leaders among us to guide and instruct us
as we prepare our families for your birth in our hearts
next Christmas,
that it will not be sugarplums that dance in our heads,
but yearning for life more abundant
and an unquenchable thirst for justice,

which cannot be attained in boxes with bows
or in any store

As we anticipate the Epiphany's festival of light,
accept our prayers for the marriages in this church,
that we might be quick to find the good in one another,
steadfast in our commitment,
eager to delight one another

We know, God,
that in the deep, dark, skeletal days of winter,
there are azalea blossoms being nourished in secret.
And so it is, too, in our relationships.

Even as we praise you
for life and its companion, death,
we also confess our utter failure
to grasp either of these mysteries in its fullness

Hear now our silent longings and petitions,
nourished in secret from the depths of our hearts:

Silent prayer

AMEN

❦ ❦ ❦ ❦

❦ New Year's Sunday and Epiphany

TEACH US TO NUMBER OUR DAYS
New Year's Sunday and Epiphany

O God of creation
who breathed the breath of life into living beings,
we come this holy day
with songs of grateful praise
for a year's new beginning

Incline your ear to us.
Accept our offerings of thanksgiving
for the possibilities of this year
stretching before us

We find ourselves, like the psalmist,
imploring you!
Teach us to number our days,
that we may apply our hearts to wisdom

Teach us to number our days,
that we may more fully live them
in the fountain of life—here and now,
relieved of boredom and fault-finding,
relieved of depleting grudges and insecurities

Teach us to number our days,
that we might taste and feel the deep beauty of the earth,
and in that tasting and in that feeling
become attentive to the sacrificial discipline
required for the care of your earth
and its peoples

Apply our hearts to the wisdom of living life more abundantly,
now, not tomorrow—
not a better day, a better time, a better place—
but now, in this small window of time,
for, like the grass, we will soon fade and wither

You know that we are tempted by other gods:
time, money, knowledge, achievement.
We are afraid, God,
that your response to us
might be the same as Jesus' response to the rich young man.
We, like him, struggle.
And, many days in this year just passed,
we have lost the fight against having other gods before you.
Forgive us

We pray for your world, for your ravaged rain forests,
your oil-polluted oceans and seas and rivers.
[List local and global ecological trouble spots]
O God of creation, we long to be gentle with your earth,
borrowing from it only what we are able to give back to it

Make us wise.
Nag at us like the widow at the judge's feet
until we say yes
to you,
to your creation,
to feeding the hungry,
comforting the sick,
welcoming the stranger

Many of us come this New Year's Sunday
with a longing,
a joy,

a falling-short-of-the-mark
that only you can hear.
Receive our silent prayers as we lift them to you:

Silent prayer

Accept these prayers
through the beloved Child
you sent to this world which you so magnificently love

Amen

❄ ❄ ❄ ❄

EMMANUEL!
WE SEARCH FOR YOU EVERYWHERE
First Sunday after Epiphany

Emmanuel!
In the passing of these days of Epiphany
the joyous heralding of angels
seems distant from us.
We search for you everywhere —
among friends and family,
along the streets,
and even among strangers

And sometimes we must confess
that like Mary and Joseph
searching for their lost son on the way home from
the Jerusalem Passover,
even when we look in the holy gathering place,
sometimes we fail to find Jesus.

We fail to see the Christ child growing.
Send forth your Spirit, O Holy One.
Remake us again to you,
that you might renew the face of the earth
and begin anew your ministry in us

Call us to be your disciples again.
We long to hear your voice
and would drop our nets
if only we were sure of its sound

Gathered here, as in an upper room,
visit us now.
Give us some assurance of your peace

Gathered here, we find a refuge under the wings
of your Spirit.
We do not feel alone.
We feel a burning inside us to be
more than we alone can be

Gathered here, we miss those who cannot be here
because they are too infirm, too stressed,
perhaps even too weary of searching for you

Some of us gather here,
knowing that we ourselves are not
good enough, honest enough, or gentle enough.
But together, we come forth
as Christians,
both in our imperfection and in our striving.
We come forth,
that we might grow along with you,

Emmanuel,
in the proclaiming of the Word,
the singing of your praise,
and the breaking of the bread

    AMEN

    ❦ ❦ ❦ ❦

IN PRAISE OF ANNAS AND SIMEONS
Second Sunday after Epiphany

In these early moments of Epiphany, God,
we remember Jesus' dedication and the ministry
of Anna and Simeon

We find ourselves compelled
to give you thanks for the Annas,
the Simeons
in our lives, in our church:
those who welcomed our mothers,
our fathers [stepparents, grandparents],
when they brought us to be dedicated in the holy place;
those who called us by name,
who rejoiced when they saw us,
who blessed us as a creation of God (and a very good one!).
They are the ones who encouraged us on the way
and taught us by example
that life is precious
and the church is a gift

In fact, God,
we believe you are love
because of those who first loved us—
those Annas and Simeons

We come here today,
seeking to become Annas and Simeons
to the children, the infants,
the families
of our church and community

We confess that we are immersed in the culture
that we often criticize.
We have fallen under its influence ourselves,
its tendency to thoughtlessness and lack of compassion.
We confess we have failed
to love children of this church, this community, this world,
as if they were
our very own children

And so, God, rejoice with us
in this day of recommitment
as we remember
that being loved deeply,
being recognized,
and being deeply known
are more valuable than the finest gold!
We long to pour out the precious oil of our lives,
anointing the children, the young adults,
who have come to this community
so that they can know
you, God,
the One who first loved

AMEN

❊ ❊ ❊ ❊

O LOVER OF SOULS
Third Sunday after Epiphany

O Holy One beyond our knowing
who loves even when we
search ourselves and find ourselves unlovable,
who heals us when we cry to you from
our souls' and our bodies'
infirmities,
O Lover of souls,
who in all our affliction is afflicted,
hear our prayers

For this world and its leaders,
we ask for strength of endurance
and fortitude of courage—
especially for those we name this morning:

> *Prayers of intercession for world leaders*
> *[List world leaders by country: China, S. Africa, Iraq, U.S., etc.]*

We ask for the safekeeping of their lives,
as ever more and more of the people of God
who on earth do dwell
in liberty and freedom
depend on such leadership

We pray for the spiritual leaders of this world, God,
and for the unknown saints
who labor in mission fields and
other world countries, bringing a cup of cool water,
clean water,
in your name.
We pray, God,
to know your mission for our lives,

those of us who labor here at home.
We thank you for work to do
and health to do it.
Show us, guide our feet and hands
to the water to be given in your name here

For life feels so short, God,
years passing as quickly in our adulthood
as a single day flew by in our childhood.
Rebuke us when we fail to stop the busy-ness at hand
and hold those we love to our hearts

Help us love one another as we would love ourselves,
listen to one another
as we would have you hear us.
Help us bear one another's burdens
as you, God, suffer when we suffer.
Forgive us our sins, God,
as we forgive those who sin against us.
Walk with us, God,
that we might discover,
as the Magi did,
that we have gifts to bring you.
Walk with us, God, that we might discover courage
to seek you out,
no matter how far the journey

In the name of the One
who came that we might have life
and have it more abundantly
we pray

AMEN

❄ ❄ ❄ ❄

WE ARE THINKING
ABOUT THOSE WISE ONES, GOD
Fourth Sunday after Epiphany

We are thinking about those wise ones, God,
who put down their lives
and left their commitments
and set out with the sky for their map

We are wondering
how wise
they were,
really.
Yet we envy them
the clarity of their task and
the obvious choice of the gifts they brought,
we long for so clear a path,
for so bright a star,
in searching out the holy.
We ache, God,
to act boldly
in regard to you,
to your Child, Jesus,
to his ministry,
and to our ministry—both as individuals and as a church.
We hunger to know the gifts we are to bring.
Reveal them to us

O God of unending mercies,
we know that Jesus was baptized by John, his cousin.
Like John,
we are surprised
that we have been chosen,

and in our hearts
we protest,
"You, Jesus, come to us?
have need of us?"

And so we find in our ordinary lives
the extraordinary news breaks in,
announcing our work:
we are called to be ordinary
cousins and family, inviting
others to dwell
with this One called Emmanuel,
the One growing in wisdom and favor before all of us.
Give us the courage
and patience to fulfill that work

May we love what is genuine,
hold fast to what is good,
love one another with mutual affection,
outdoing one another in showing honor,
rejoicing in hope
while we persevere in prayer

AMEN

❊ ❊ ❊ ❊

RELEASE OUR STIFF NECKS
Fifth Sunday after Epiphany

O God of deliverance,
we stand before you
with Abraham

and command of you:
"Shall not the judge of all the earth do right?"

Listen to our prayers for peace.
Gather them into yourself and
multiply them like fishes and loaves.
Light them into tongues of Pentecost fire,
so they might scorch this earth with light,
until that which can weave evil within each of our hearts
is defeated—
and never again
will violence or trespass be committed
by one child of God against another.
We beseech you,
God of mercy,
be merciful,
save us from ourselves.
Do not turn your ear from us.
We beseech you,
God of mercy,
hear our prayers for our enemies;
bless them
and do not curse them

Release our stiff necks,
so that
we yearn to change our lives,
as eager to repent
as we are to do justice

We come today
as every day,
utterly defeated when the innocent suffer.

Especially today we remember
all innocent suffering children:

Prayers of intercession

We come hungry for relationship with you, God,
knowing not where to begin
but with our own restless hearts

For the promise of the sun
in the midst of winter's harshness,
for the miracle of being invited
to love and care for one another,
and for the work of prayer,
we gratefully end our petitions to you

Amen

❉ ❉ ❉ ❉

LIGHT AND FLAVOR
Sixth Sunday after Epiphany

God of wisdom,
in these weeks of Epiphany
we have journeyed with Jesus
from his dedication as a baby
to his preaching tour and
acts of healing

We have found that it is easier to love Mary's
baby in a manger
than it is to conform our lives

to the difficult teachings
of that grown-up man and rabbi
who commanded us to be salt and light to the world,
so that all will recognize
our abiding love of you, God,
and themselves be drawn in love to you,
Creating and Sustaining One

Yet we must confess, God.
Forgive us and turn us around as we admit
our struggle, sometimes failing
to retain our flavor and light,
in our culture where
we are unnerved with distractions

We remember that your Child, a grown-up man,
taught us through example
that ministry
and the work of salt and light
are sustained through solitude and silence,
as he went alone to the mountain
or into the boat across the water
or simply to a lonely place
to pray, to listen, to be restored

And so we pray today, God,
for the courage
and the self-discipline
to pursue silence and solitude,
to sit in utter quiet and loneliness,
listening for your voice,
that we might be refreshed
enough

to turn our hearts back to the
care of souls and bodies
of children and infirm,
bringing flavor and light,
bearing our love for you with all our
heart, mind, soul, and strength

AMEN

❧ ❧ ❧ ❧

AS ONE HAVING AUTHORITY
Seventh Sunday after Epiphany

God,
as we watch
your Child's life
unfold from childhood to adult ministry,
we have more questions
than the stories
and parables
and teachings
answer

We are frustrated by the distance
of time and space
between the words that Mark and Matthew and Luke
gave to us
and the experience we long to have
of meeting, knowing,
touching
Jesus
ourselves

We want to have heard
Jesus as he boldly entered
the synagogue on the Sabbath and taught as
one having authority.
We know that is how we are to teach and speak
as Christians.
We needed to hear it,
to be instructed by it,
to model our words and actions by it,
so that people are astounded by what they see—
how we love one another,
the integrity, the authority of our lives and living—
and they come to ask us
about this Jesus the Christ
and the life more abundant which he holds out

Why must we drink this
living water,
carried across such a distance of time and space
that only
a drop
reaches
our parched
souls?

God, give us
whatever
it takes,
whatever
we need.
Enter our lives and rebuke whatever unclean
spirit
lives there,

so that we
can be sustained
and refreshed
by even
a
drop

AMEN

❦ ❦ ❦ ❦

O YAHWEH, TEACH US YOUR PATHS
Last Sunday after Epiphany

O God of tenderness and enduring compassion,
we are bewildered in this world
by our violence and callousness toward one another,
and we are afflicted
by our careless acts of selfishness against your earth.
We come, God,
confused and unconsoled.
We come, God,
uncertain of ourselves, full of self-doubt.
We come, God, to hear your words of reassurance

Your love shall never leave us
nor your covenant be shaken,
for you are Yahweh,
whose thirsty, impoverished servants
receive water,
grain,
and milk and honey

O Faithful One,
forgive us when we
spend ourselves and our time and our money
on what fails to satisfy

Have mercy, O Merciful One, on our gifts to you,
that they may satisfy
thirst and hunger,
that they may bring blessing and glory and honor
to you, O Most Unfathomable

We long to know your ways, O Yahweh.
Teach us your paths,
that we may comfort the lonely,
seek out the outcast,
and welcome the sojourner

Hear now our innermost longings
as we silently bring our petitions to you:

Silent prayer

God, in your mercy
hear our prayers

AMEN

❀ ❀ ❀ ❀

BREAK THROUGH
OUR ORDINARY LIVES, GOD
Transfiguration Sunday

On this most amazing day of
dazzling transfiguration,
we confess immediately, God,
that we, like Peter,
want to make holy things manageable.
We want to build booths and bottle what
dazzles

Forgive us as we tromp through mysteries,
trying to press them into formulaic doctrinal truths
and scientific certainty

We simply don't know
where to turn in the face of such blinding,
astounding events,
and so we feel the poverty of our spirit
in the same moment we feel our minds
resisting today's story

Perhaps that transfiguring light
was about purifying
and cleansing
what had become, through living,
dust-covered and
ordinary

Break through the ordinary
in our lives, God of mystery.

Purify and cleanse.
Reveal the inconceivable to us
as you did to our brother Peter

We bring before you the brokenness of our lives,
the smallness we feel before your acts of creation.
We confess our desire, like Peter's,
to build a tabernacle and
stay
at the top of the mountain
alone with Jesus

Encourage us, God.
Help us
as we begin the slow descent down that mountain
with Jesus
to feed those who are hungry,
to practice hospitality with those who are not easily loved,
and to be the good news of life more abundant

God, in your mercy,
hear our prayers on behalf of those who suffer today.
Show us the way to them
and to the mystery of your presence there:

Prayers of intercession

AMEN

❦ ❦ ❦ ❦

❧ Lent

ABIDE WITH US IN PATIENCE
First Sunday in Lent

O Spirit of God who drove Jesus into the desert,
we come,
a Lenten people,
longing for the urgent moving of the Spirit among us,
praying for courage to be driven by your Spirit
even into the wilderness for forty days and nights

In your mercy for us, God,
send the insistent power of your Spirit,
so that as winter gives way to the warmth of spring,
we, too, can peel away whatever is inessential or
false in ourselves,
our communities,
our church

Some of us come to you knowing the fatigue of a burden
that will not be lifted,
the pain of an illness that will not succumb to healing,
the weary path of a loneliness whose ache cannot be
dulled.
We wish, like the psalmist, for wings like a dove,
that we could fly away.
But where can we go but to you?
For you are our comfort, our refuge, our strength

Some of us come with a joy so full that this time of Lent
feels a little distant.
We hum songs of praise for the coming of springtime,
anticipating crocuses and new families being born.
We pray for wisdom as we, your holy people,
clap our hands and shout for joy

Yet we also approach you with hushed quiet this morning, God,
wondering how we can welcome the stranger, feed the hungry
in this impoverished and hungry world.
Hear our prayers for all your children who have known the
devastation of natural disasters;
for those affected by:
[List local and global floods, tornadoes, earthquakes, spring storms]

We remember our missionaries;
make their ministry as the fishes and loaves:
*[List the names of your denomination's missionaries and
where they serve]*

Move among us this Lent, O God.
Remind us again of the mustard seed—
the smallest of all seeds on earth,
but when sown, it grows like a weed,
putting forth shelter
for the birds to find shade and rest

Plant that ineradicable mustard seed within us
and accept our prayers of longing for your presence

AMEN

✻ ✻ ✻ ✻

HEARTS AND HANDS
AND EARS OPEN
Second Sunday in Lent

O God of love,
whose Spirit stirred over the waters of chaos
and called forth light into being,
we gather in this morning's light,
in the warmth of this community,
your Spirit stirring among us,
calling us, cradling us,
until we say,
"Yes,
we are your people.
Yes,
we will be light
in this creation of yours"

Reveal to us, then, in this Lenten season,
the faith of
Sarah and Abraham—
faith firm enough
to hear when you speak,
even when it means releasing the comfort of security,
leaving what we know
and walking into the unknown,
the new challenge,
to follow you,
to be your people

Guide us, God,
here in this church.
Shape us so that Sarah and Abraham

would recognize themselves here:
hearts and hands and ears open
to being in relationship with you,
giving thanks to you in all things,
even in the midst of one another's burdens,
so that we may bear them together,
knowing the lightness of a load
when so many of our brothers' and sisters' hands
lift it with us

We are here this morning,
eager for you to reveal to us
a love that hopes all things
and endures all things

Even the burden of a love
that sometimes says no,
a love that hopes all things
even in the midst of loneliness

We pray to live a love that endures even the misery of failure,
that transcends the temptation of judgment
and forgives as quickly
as we would have others forgive us

We pray now for those among us and our families who are ill,
who know pain and grief,
that as we move among their struggle with illness,
we may be instruments of Christ's peace,
bringing comfort in Christ's name:

Prayers of intercession

We praise you for this day
and the miracle of senses to live it,
for you alone are God.
Accept our grateful thanks, O God of steadfast love.
We offer it with our whole hearts

And now with so great a cloud of witnesses
as to run with perseverance the race that is set before us,
we pause
in silence,
listening to you:

Silent prayer

AMEN

❋ ❋ ❋ ❋

OUR SOULS LONG FOR PEACE
Third Sunday in Lent

O God of all,
we bring our restless hearts
to you this Lent,
our souls longing for peace ... peace.
Yet there is no peace

Like the woman at the well,
we are amazed at all you know about us;
like her,
we long for the refreshment of your comfort;
and, like her,
we chafe against a past that binds us

She did not understand Jesus' words
although she was thirsty.
We, too, struggle
with the mystery of those promised living waters
and what they might mean for our lives

We confess to you this morning
that, like the Israelites, we are prone
to a weakness for other gods;
that sometimes we are very religious about our jobs,
our activities,
our entertainment

We confess that when we write out our daily lists of
priorities,
you are absent.
We confess that, like Paul,
we fail in doing the good we want

We confess, God,
that this Lenten path we are walking
is a difficult one.
We have celebrated the birth of your Child
and have warmly held him in our hearts during Advent.
We joyfully marked the days of Epiphany,
but as we anticipate taking those first steps toward Palm
Sunday,
we are full of sorrow.
We walk slowly, God,
with dragging feet.
We do not want Jesus to die

We pray for faith
like the faith of the woman

who struggled to grasp the hem of Jesus' garment
and was healed,
faith enough to
stand at the foot of a cross

For we come this morning,
striving to respond to your gifts to us,
as eager to be your people in the world
through using those gifts
as we are needful of receiving them

Show us the path, God.
Make clear the way

    AMEN

    ❈ ❈ ❈ ❈

YOUR LOVE PERSISTS, STUBBORNLY, WARMLY
Fourth Sunday in Lent

O God, who so loved the world
that you sent your only, beloved Child,
we come to you this morning
trying to fully understand that you love us still—
regardless of who we are or are not,
what we have done or left undone,
regardless of what we are capable or incapable of doing.
Your love persists, stubbornly, warmly
welcoming us back to you

We come with hearts humming grateful praise to you
for the signs that life continues—
the hope of newborn buds on trees,
the promise of daffodils rising from winter graves,
the fragrant nourishing mist of rain

We come with hearts of grateful praise,
some of us weary, others refreshed,
praising you in the midst of time's swift passing.
And as we live in these passing days of Lent,
we begin to restlessly consider
(like flowers responding to the sun's kiss)
your Lenten call to us
for transformation

For such a possibility of transformation
we are grateful to your grace,
which releases us from any falsehood or pretensions
of who we may imagine ourselves to be
and invites us to be what we are—
human,
forgiven,
set free

You, O God of transforming love,
suffer when your children suffer.
You know some of us come this morning
with the heaviness of a sorrow
.that cannot be lifted except through you.
You know our hearts,
our prayers,
before we can speak them.
Embrace our loved ones who are sick:

Walk with us,
that we are mindful to walk closely with one another
when we suffer from loneliness, uncertainty, disappointment

Still our fears, God; quiet them until we hear again
your voice, steady and familiar,
lifting us to you

Teach us your way of faithfulness,
that we may be careful in our relationships,
growing always in love
and desire
for your presence

AMEN

❋ ❋ ❋ ❋

HOW IS IT THAT THE POOR IN SPIRIT ARE BLESSED?
Fifth Sunday in Lent

We come these days of Lent
wondering, God,
how it is that the poor in spirit are blessed
and that theirs is the realm of heaven.
Lead us, then, to poverty of spirit.
Lead us in the way of storing up treasure
which moths and rust cannot destroy
nor thieves break in and steal

Hear our prayers this morning
for the families of the world,
those who have received news that would
mark the breaking point
and chase a family into corners of anxiety
and enmity one against the other.
We pray for families of children who are ill
and for those who are fighting for life.
We pray for parents who suffer
with their children who suffer:

Prayers of intercession

O God,
though you are with us every moment,
we confess
we are sometimes driven away from you
when, undone by grief,
we wonder if we might never be put back together again
after the death of a child
or spouse
or brother, sister, or parent

We come to glimpse the suffering which you, God,
endured
through
your Child's suffering

Accept our silent prayers of confession
for the times we have failed
to respond
to such wondrous love as this—
that a parent so loved the world,

an only child was shared
who scandalized us
with his outrageous acts of compassion and healing:

Silent prayer

We implore you, God, for your mercy,
bathing us in forgiveness for what we have failed to do.
We pray God, for your mercy
as we try
to love one another.
Do not give up on us

We ask all these things, God,
longing, like the psalmist,
for the coming age,
where mercy and faithfulness meet,
when faithfulness shall spring from the earth
and justice look down from heaven

AMEN

✻ ✻ ✻ ✻

CHILDREN WAVING PALMS FOR JOY
Palm Sunday

O God of glory,
as the stones themselves
would call out your praise,
we, too, come this morning
with hosannas,

adding our human voices to your creation's chorus and
the heavens
telling your glory

Accept our joy,
our hearts overflowing.
We praise you, holy Wise One,
for the gift of children waving palms

Accept, too,
our anguish
that our misguided human dreams of the Messiah's realm
led us from hosannas and waving palm branches
to, only days later,
shouting for Jesus' crucifixion

Forgive the hubris of our imagining
that we might not have been like all the others,
either in fickle waving of palms
or falling asleep at prayer in the garden

In our hearts we know that
before the cock crowed three times,
we in the church pew—
just like the rock on which Christ founded the church—
would deny Jesus three times
to protect our terrified
selves

Hear our prayers for those who suffer today,
where each of us ultimately suffers—
alone

For the pain of human lives,
constricted to a grid of circumstances beyond their control,
God, hear our prayer

For those who suffer the constraints
of unfulfilling, deadening work;
for those whose work is largely invisible,
God, hear our prayer

Turn the stones of defeat at Gethsemane and Golgotha
to the active compassion of prayer,
bringing to life
that which is asleep

For you are gracious, O Lover of souls

AMEN

❊ ❊ ❊ ❊

Easter and Eastertide

O GOD OF EASTER
Easter Sunday

O God of new life,
hear our joyful noise to you
as we come into your presence with singing,
for Christ
is risen.

On this morning when the heavens and earth are telling
your glory,
when the earth itself would cry out,
we gather together—
brothers and sisters in Christ—
remembering
the first Easter morning,
when three women,
hands heavy with spices of sadness,
sought the living among the dead
and were astounded to find an empty tomb.

We come this morning
as Easter people,
radiant from the joy of what we have come here
to proclaim again this morning:
Christ is risen!

We come this morning recalling Christ's tomb
because it is a place
where Christ is no longer found—
but God's presence
and newness of life are.
We come

to speak the resurrection,
Christ is risen,
so that we ourselves become children of grace,
the stones that entomb us rolling away

We come
to speak the resurrection,
Christ is risen,
as we ourselves—disciples of Christ—
heed our call to roll away the stones that entomb others

God, we remember on this Easter morning of light
your children throughout this earth
who are suffering from illness, hunger, violence,
the struggle of aging, and the wounds of a loneliness
no human touch can heal.
Our hearts overflow.
Hear our silent prayers:

    Silent prayer

As we seek new beginnings this Easter,
we ask these prayers in the name of the Resurrected One

    AMEN

    ❀ ❀ ❀ ❀

AN EASTER PEOPLE
Second Sunday of Easter

O Beloved One,
in your wondrous love

we find our moving and being.
Incline your ear.
Incline your ear to your people
as we raise our voices to you,
joining in the chorus of your creation
in its song of glory to you, the Breath of life

As we feel the earth moving toward spring's warmth,
our hearts, too, grow warm
and return longingly to you,
wholly thankful
for the miracle of the empty tomb.
Receive them.
Reshape them

We come before you
frustrated and confused
that so many across the earth's face
cannot worship together this morning without
the fear of suffering and death

Write on our hearts
what rolling away the stones of our brothers' and sisters'
tombs of oppression
requires of us.
Humble us to your wisdom, O Holy One,
for if you record our sins,
who can survive?
Deliver us,
deliver us, merciful God

For your yoke is easy
and your burden is light

Tender God,
grant us full pardon,
for you are slow to anger, rich in love

Some of us come here this morning
starving for the comfort of a community,
only to discover a deepened sense of aloneness.
Rain down the comfort of your Spirit,
for our souls ache for you
and they will not rest
until they rest again in you

We bring before you the beloved among us who are ill,
even as our love for them
calls us
to pray for all your children who suffer.
Embrace them with your comfort, your peace:

Prayers of intercession

As the scent of Easter lilies
lingers in this space,
we remember vividly
that we are the people of the promise.
An Easter people,
we bring ourselves to you
as we bring these prayers
thanking you for the gift of your Child,
in whose name and ministry
we pray

AMEN

❀ ❀ ❀ ❀

THE FRAGILE LOVE THAT
GENTLY HOLDS US
Third Sunday of Easter

O God,
wholly Divine One
who knew us before we were in the womb,
how we long to be fully known
now,
here,
in this moment

We feel Easter
and the glory of you
all around us.
But it is sometimes easier to celebrate a babe in Mary's arms
or to mourn our Rabbi's death on a cross
than it is each day to walk faithfully in the new life
of resurrection

O Wondrous One,
we ache for you
in the promise of spring,
when we catch the warming sun
in our hearts.
Still,
we ache for you like a dry and weary land

Come, know us.
Let us be revealed
to ourselves and to one another
through your knowing of us.

Surely, you are revealed, Holy One,
through the fragile web of love that gently holds each of us

In these Easter days of resurrection,
we remember the friends gone before,
who, if we listen, breathe the spirit of life among us still—
saints who raised the roof of this church
to the nurture of the reign of God
and for the care of the least of these

We pray for our children this morning.
Thanking you for their faces, which reflect the world's
wonder to us,
revealing to us surprisingly candid photographs of us—
their parents, teachers, and church

Let us become like them,
quick to reveal hurt feelings, disappointments, and sorrows
with the rapid deepening of love
that comes in the healing.
Give us ears to hear the wisdom of our children.
Give us courage to speak our hurt quickly and
unaccusingly, eager for restored relationship

Like the widow before the judge,
remind us incessantly
to tell our children
the story of their ancestors in this church,
who loved them before they were born
and raised this church for them.
Let us tell our children over and over
and over again
that we love them,

until they trust that love
and can believe that you love them, too

Hear our prayers for those absent from us
who know the hush of pain in hospitals
and the anguish of those who grieve.
Send your Spirit
to quicken the healing

Give us grace and courage and boldness,
that we might follow the example of the women
at the foot of the cross,
so that we, too, are present
when our brothers and sisters suffer

Our hearts were made for you, God.
Silently now we lift them to you:

   Silent prayer

   AMEN

   ✹ ✹ ✹ ✹

MERCIFUL GOD, YOU TURNED THE SEA INTO DRY LAND
Fourth Sunday of Easter

Merciful God, you turned the sea into dry land
so that your people, once held captive,
were free at last.
We come this morning,

praying for solid ground to tread on
in the midst of a sea of burdens
which would hold us captive

Steady our steps

Even as we praise you for the hope of being reborn at
Easter,
we come carrying old wounds which eclipse
the possibility of new birth
and keep us on unsteady ground.
Help us lay those old hurts down

We gather before you this morning,
as every morning,
in a tangle of human relationships,
sisters and brothers in Christ,
whose love for one another
helps us to understand the incomprehensible—
your love for us—
and whose challenge to us
sends us back again and again
to the call of loving you with all our
heart, mind, soul, and strength

We come, perhaps most grateful of all
for this human community and its forgiveness,
for through being forgiven,
we learn to forgive ourselves
and others

As we prepare for the spring to come
we discover a homesickness,

a longing to see and feel the warmth
of the beloved faces we are separated from
either through life
or through death

We pray for those people who are absent,
whom we carry in our hearts.
We praise you for the hope of reunion

As the days promise to grow gentle,
we anticipate the new life of Easter.
Our hearts turn to the ill,
the bereaved,
the suffering.
Listen, God,
to our silent prayers:

Silent prayer

Even as we praise you for the beauty of the earth,
we feel your judgment for our careless
abuse of it.
Forgive us

We bring these longings,
confessions,
and praises before you,
whose justice and mercy
will flow down like rivers.
Let it be, God. Let it be

AMEN

❁ ❁ ❁ ❁

O GOD OF SECOND CHANCES
Fifth Sunday of Easter

O God of second chances,
we thank you for the severe mercy
brought to our souls
when, convicted of our own falling short of the mark,
we seek out forgiveness,
speaking the sin we have committed

For the Spirit's persistent ministry among us,
chastening until we respond to the call to repentance,
and for the miraculous possibility of
turning around,
trying again,
we are amazed

And we are hopeful
that if we can,
with the conviction of the Spirit,
speak out our sins and walk away from them,
nations can, too;
that if we
are able to seek forgiveness of one another
and speak to the ones against whom we have sinned,
naming our sins against them,
nations can, too.
For in this season of Easter,
we remember that ashes we were
and to ashes we will return again.
We are reminded of the forgiveness granted
the prodigal child and arrogant older brother,
hoping that such grace will be ours

We would like the faith of a mustard seed,
so as to move mountains,
but ask today simply for the faith to go
to those who suffer in heart or mind,
the faith to be like the Marys at the foot of the cross,
providing compassionate presence for those who suffer.
We pray for the tenacity and tenderness
to search out the hidden hurt in one another
like the woman searching for her lost coin

For we live in a broken hearted world, God,
and we live for the fulfillment of your promise
that you will bind up the hurt of your people

On this morning,
we thank you for your fulfilled promise among us,
Jesus the Christ,
sent to the brokenhearted,
sent
to
us

 Amen

 ❧ ❧ ❧ ❧

GIVE US A WORD, O GOD
Sixth Sunday of Easter

God of all seasons,
we come this Eastertide
up to our elbows
in commitments and conflictedness

We are relieved to hear
of a love that repairs,
resurrects,
restores

Our own stories
of our own lives
are full of unexpected changes in direction and course.
We end up in places we never intended to be,
through no fault of our own
but through the connective tissue
of love

Our prayers this morning, God,
are spoken from the strength and fragility
of that connective tissue,
which brings life
and form
to what was merely a tomb of dry bones

Thank you for the possibility
of repairing what is damaged

Thank you for the possibility
of rewriting our lives within the template
of stories of Jesus.
Thank you for the possibility
of being born again this Easter

God, you know that we spend a lot of time
on ourselves
in this church.
There is much that must be done,

but we know that life more abundant
does not reside in an error-free newsletter
or a flawless children's program

Life more abundant
is in the discipline,
the wisdom,
the work,
the prayer,
the study,
and the life and death
of Jesus

As we labor over membership roles
and attend to bereavement dinners,
as we clean and diaper the littlest ones among us,
as we visit those whose homes have become their church,
give us a word, God.
Give us a word to speak,
that we might bring the flavor of salt
and the warmth of light
in your world

AMEN

❀ ❀ ❀ ❀

THE LIVING WATER OF WORSHIP
Seventh Sunday of Easter

We gather in the assembly, God,
anxious to be
together again,

re-membering the body of Christ,
desiring in our presence to one another
your presence,
your body.
Like Thomas,
we want to touch your hands, your side,
your feet

For we feel vulnerable, O God,
and human,
and our need of you is great

For the gift of life
and its goodness,
we give you thanks.
For the wisdom in which to live it,
we ask your revelation

For the miracle of your church
and for our faith community,
[name of your church],
where anytime
one of us suffers,
all of us suffer—
we ask for health and time
to give back,
as we are able,
what has been given to us here

We are moved by the sorrow and pain
of those with whom we live and have our being
in this church.

They have become faces of Christ to us,
encouraging and challenging us
when we are turned away from your Spirit

We remember the blind man who washed
and was reborn in body and spirit.
Like him, we need to wash
in the healing waters of Siloam

Make of our worship
a pool of life-giving water,
bearing your presence,
your peace

Make of this time that we share together
a sacred center
that orders all our working
and all our cares
to your holy end

AMEN

❋ ❋ ❋ ❋

GOD OF MIRACLES
Pentecost
Baptism

O God of miracles
of Pentecost wind
and baptismal waters,
we rejoice

this morning
in being called
your people.
We thank you for
the young lives added to our community today—
Timothys and Phoebes.
. we are grateful for the gifts they bring

Accept our prayers of gratitude
. for the families and friends
who have nurtured them.
Make of us a community worthy of receiving them,
living by the example of our lives
how to be gospel people in thought, word, and action

Even in the midst of such wondrous joy,
we remember today those who,
bewildered,
feel their lives dashed against the rocks.
We pray for those who know the
anguish of being abused.
We pray for marriages
both fragile and strong,
young and old.
We pray for each one of us who
one day at a time
achieves sobriety,
restoring equilibrium to our lives

We pray particularly for our church
and your church throughout the world
today, God.

Not bold enough to beseech you for tongues of fire
dancing
on our heads,
we are nonetheless bold enough to demand that
you fill us again
with the living, refreshing wind of the Spirit

May we become
the refreshing wind of the Spirit
in our world,
feeding the hungry,
writing a letter to the lonely,
visiting the imprisoned,
clothing those who are exposed

Let it be, God. Let it be

   AMEN

   ❧ ❧ ❧ ❧

COME DOWN, LOVE DIVINE
Pentecost (Alternate)

O God, in whom we have our breath and our being,
we come to praise you,
a group of believers
gathered in one place
in Christ's name

We come confessing that many times our eyes
have not been looking
for your tongues of fire.

Our hearts have not been open to being filled.
Our gifts have not been used generously

Descend upon us, Holy Spirit, that our lives
and this church
reflect your presence among us.
Come down, O Love Divine,
that we may be able to pray together
and understand what we are saying,
that we may feed the hungry together,
doing justice, loving mercy, walking humbly with you
together

Make us your church
through the rush of wind and burn of fire.
Rain your fire among us.
Make us the church,
re-form us—
because we have neither courage nor human strength enough
to become what you have called us to be.
Come down, O Love Divine,
to those who have given their consent
for your action in their lives this morning

We live in daily wonder and gratitude
and joy of being baptized into the church,
the whole people of God.
We praise you, O God, for the newness of a life
shaped by Christ

AMEN

❊ ❊ ❊ ❊

❧ *Ordinary Time*

BATHE OUR WITHERED SPIRITS
IN YOUR LIVING WATERS
First Sunday in Ordinary Time

O Creating and Sustaining One
whose Spirit stirred over the waters
and created light and life,
we have come this holy morning
with hearts and hands and voices
aching for your presence,
waiting to be gathered in you.
Move among us;
bathe our withered spirits in your living waters

For the miracle of life
and the love of one another,
we are eternally grateful.
For it is in the touch of a loved one,
the healing laughter of friends;
it is in the conversation
whose tenderness lies far beyond words,
binding soul to soul,
that we begin to understand
your abiding friendship

We come,
afraid for this world's well-being,
praying for peace,
even as we confess to you
that it is so difficult—
yea, some days impossible—to live peacefully,
even within our own families and neighborhoods.
Forgive us.

We long, God, to be transformed
in our relationships,
especially here in your church,
that earthen vessels with feet of clay might be able
to follow the One who brings peace

Give to us
a love that is genuine
and a watchfulness in our relationships
that honors and remembers your presence among us

We remember today those who grieve,
especially those who have lost loved ones
in the violence of our world.
We recall places of conflict, at home and abroad:
[list local and global places of conflict].
Above the noise of gunfire,
give us ears to hear
the cries of Rachel weeping for her children

Hear our prayers for the suffering and sick,
even as we also pray for those
who watch and wait with them:

Prayers of intercession

Comfort them,
for you will wipe away every tear from our eyes.
Let it be, God,
let it be

AMEN

❋ ❋ ❋ ❋

HOLD OUR LIVES QUIETLY
Second Sunday in Ordinary Time

O Creating God,
even as we praise you for the beauty of the earth,
for the glory of the skies,
every year we are reminded
of the power of your creation—
through the floods and destructive storms of spring,
the unpredicted violence of an earthquake's tear through
the earth,
fires that annually consume thousands of acres of forest

In a world where time speeds by so rapidly
and tomorrow is taken for granted,
appointment books, semester schedules, and deadlines
seem to rule our lives.
We are reawakened now
to the reign of God in our midst.
We become attentive now
to hear your still voice,
and we pause and hold our lives quietly,
praying for a heart of wisdom

You have searched us and known us, O God.
You know the hurt we hide behind our eyes,
the bewilderment of our hearts.
Hear our supplication for your comfort,
your presence
in our families,
in your families through this earth

We thank you for work to do.

We thank you, God, for challenge.
We praise you for life and the ability
to labor as you have called us to labor

Hear our prayers of thanksgiving for this community
and the lightened load we come to know
through bearing one another's burdens

We implore you, God,
that those who suffer may receive relief;
that you will journey with us
as we visit the sick,
feed the hungry,
clothe the vulnerable,
and comfort the disconsolate

AMEN

❀ ❀ ❀ ❀

WE PRAY FOR FATHERS
Third Sunday in Ordinary Time
Father's Day

To the One who
satisfies those who are thirsty
and fills the hungry with good things,
we come
longing for unmistakable signs
of you,
envious of what the Israelites knew
through pillar of fire and desert bursting into
streams.

We come to you today,
many of us as fathers,
every one of us a father's child.
We come wanting
to be all we can be to one another,
both as fathers
and as fathers' children.
We come frustrated when our expectations of one another
leave us hurt and disappointed
instead of mutually cherished

We pray for fathers today—
young, old, and those who have died.
May they be worthy of honor
and blessed by their own children

We pray for fathers
strong in faith,
firm in limits,
hearty in love and laughter,
and full of grace;
fathers who,
when their child asks for bread,
will not give them a stone.
We pray for lightened burdens today
for all fathers,
that they may enjoy the challenge and the delight
of their children.
Anoint every father this day
with the virtues of constancy and perseverance

Take our prayers swiftly to
wherever on this earth
anyone is unjustly sacrificed, hurt,
for whatever reasons—political, economic, racial, ideological

Give us courage
to pay the costs
of being advocates
for your creation,
your earth,
your oceans,
and for human rights for all peoples who on earth do dwell

We remember, God, the ones who are absent from us.
We pray for their renewal
of mind, body, and spirit
and for safe journeys home to us

We remember the sick,
the aging,
the very young,
asking that you—
knowing our every need
before we speak it—
will comfort and steady
those who cry out to you.
We bring our silent prayers of intercession and petition to you:

Silent prayer

AMEN

❧ ❧ ❧ ❧

FOR THE INEXPRESSIBLE
GIFT OF BEING ALIVE!
Fourth Sunday in Ordinary Time

For the
inexpressible gift
of being alive—
eyes that can see,
mouths that can speak,
ears to hear—
we are grateful to you,
O Creating God!

For the magnificent gift
of those we love;
for the laughter
and the sorrow
of being together,
even when we fail
to love one another as we should—
even then, God;
for the unmatched gift
of loving and being loved,
we are grateful to you,
O Sustaining One

Because we would have you
surround us as tangibly
as our own skin;
because we would have you
embrace us
as our own loved ones
and speak to us

words of admonition
and rebuke
and love;
because we want to
hear your voice,
we are here this morning,
O Mysterious and Hidden One

Because each of us
wants to know herself or himself
as a member of the body
of Christ,
whose birth and life and death and resurrection
we remember today;
because we worship and sing and pray and live
in the name of your Child,
we have come here today

Because there are parts of us that are unacceptable,
unlovable,
weak,
and full of betrayal,
we are here, God.
Forgive in us
what we are unable to forgive
in ourselves.
Because there are injuries
that each of us carries,
damage done to us by others,
physical, mental, emotional;
because we seek reparation
and healing,
we come,
O Repairing One

Because when we sing together
our hands and feet and minds
are enthused to do your work,
we are here this morning
to sing for you

Thanks be to you, O God,
for the gift of being here

AMEN

❦ ❦ ❦ ❦

GOD'S MANY NAMES
Fifth Sunday in Ordinary Time

God of many names,
our Rock and Redeemer,
Sustainer and Friend,
we gather before you
and find ourselves amazed
with a sweet joy
that here in this place,
we are equal before you—
social workers, lawyers,
singers or pray-ers, mothers,
teachers or librarians,
unemployed or retired

Here,
in this sacred space and time,
with all our different names
and occupations

and histories,
remarkably we are all
equivalent—
baptized,
broken,
in need of you

Reveal yourself to us
through the stories of our ancestors.
Speak to us through Phoebe and Barnabas,
through Lydia and Timothy.
Move us through their stories,
that we might discover,
O God,
what ministry is ours to do

And having found
what is ours to do,
bless us, that we might have the strength
to fulfill it

We come this day,
some of us mourning untimely death,
the loss of health and strength;
some of us heart-heavy and regretful over lost time,
misspent in wounding relationships

Some of us come here this morning having
entered the anguished night of the soul,
angry with you, God,
angry with ourselves,
weary from suffering

Our desire is that our suffering end,
and our prayer is that you abide with us in it.
Accept the whisper of gratitude from our lips
for the people of our church,
[name your church],
through whom we know care and nurture
and comfort
and challenge

Make us able to receive the multitude of gifts
offered by this faith community,
as you write your many names
on our hearts

AMEN

❧ ❧ ❧ ❧

TO YOU! O CREATING ONE, WHO KNIT US TOGETHER
Sixth Sunday in Ordinary Time

To you! O Creating One
who knit us together in our mothers' wombs,
be gracious and receive our prayer of praise,
for you have done marvelous things.
You, O Most High, have heard our supplications
and delivered release to the captive

For we see your redemptive movement in human hearts
throughout the world

and throughout the world's peoples.
We sing a new song unto you,
for we have waited, God,
waited and hoped in you.
Hear our prayers this morning for your church
throughout the world
and for our denomination and its leaders:
*[list general minister, bishop, regional minister, or district
superintendent by name].*
We ask for your strength of purpose
and the wisdom of Solomon for our clergy and lay leaders.
Reassure them in their ministries;
guide them when perplexed.

Prayers of intercession

Hear our prayers for absent friends and loved ones
who face hardship and fear
far away from their families,
their homes.
Hold them with your strong and outstretched arms
when we are unable to do so

We pray for our families,
that we may be steadfast and wise,
giving comfort when needed,
seeking comfort in our own time of need,
fulfilling the commitments we have made,
respecting healthy boundaries and limits
in one another

We pray for your family across this earth, God;
for the lonely and the isolated, longing to hear words of welcome;
for the grieving and the ill, who struggle for healing and pain's end.
For you, O God of transforming love,
suffer when your human creation suffers.
Walk with us,
that we may be mindful
to walk closely with one another

Hear now the silent prayers and longings of our hearts
as we bring them to you:

Silent prayer

We ask these things
in the love that hopes all things,
endures all things

AMEN

※ ※ ※ ※

WE FEEL CAUGHT BETWEEN EXILE AND PILGRIMAGE
Seventh Sunday in Ordinary Time

O fathomless Mystery,
our lives unfold
like the grass of the field;
we flourish and fade—
the shape and end of our own lives
as great a mystery to us as you are, O God—
for we cannot know tomorrow
or even
the events of this day's fulfillments,
yet the passing of time
brings all things
new

And so we gather this morning,
the body of Christ,
crying out our thanks to you
for all good gifts
through which you have visited your people

We thank you
for the lives
of those who have gone before us
here
and for the ones that will come after.
And on this day
of praise,
we thank you, God,
that the One whom you called and kept and blessed
and sent to us
has begun good work in us

We confess, O Holy One,
that in this passage of our life together,
we feel caught between exile and pilgrimage—
yet you call the leaven
of your Word in us
to rise.
You call us
closer to your mystery

In you,
the Source of strength,
we wait now,
hopeful that we might
sustain one another,
united in spirit,
looking after others' interests as we do our own,
recognizing the child of God
in ourselves,
in others.
Let us be children of God in everything we do

We remember those separated from us
for the refreshment of vacation.
Bless them in their journey,
that they may return to us
restored.
We remember those separated from us this morning
by illness and age.
Be a lamp unto our feet
as we seek them out

We speak to you,
desiring that our lives
be
a
prayer

Hear our silent longings and thanksgivings.
In our silence
we wait for you, O God:

Silent prayer

AMEN

❊ ❊ ❊ ❊

RESTORE OUR SOULS, RENEW A RIGHT SPIRIT WITHIN US
Eighth Sunday in Ordinary Time

We understand
it is in the simple things
that we find you, God:
a moment's quiet,
the reassuring voice of a friend,
the mystery of the earth's seasons

But our lives
feel complicated and
at a great distance from such simplicity

We wonder how it is that the
meek shall inherit the earth;

we wonder what that means for our lives
in the midst of striving for achievement

You promised that
those who seek will find;
we are seekers, God,
and we ask that you reveal to us
the mystery of being meek

We thank you for work to do—
even when it means faithful acts of kindness
for a church building,
or taking the pile of towels in the church kitchen home to
launder,
or the unromantic work of disinfecting all those nursery toys

We learn from the youngest among us,
especially in the tedious, repetitive questions
of the four-year-olds in our church:
"Why is the grass green?"
"Why is the sky blue?"

We see our own selves reflected through their queries
as we ask questions of you, God, repeatedly,
imploring you:
"Why do the innocent suffer?"
"Is it something we have done?"
"Is it something we have failed to do?"
"What is the cause of this suffering?"

Many of us are here this morning, God,
in the fervent hope
that here

we have found
a sacred space
where Christ will say to any who would accuse
or judge us:
"You who are without sin, cast the first stone"

And so our fists are unclenched;
we drop our stone.
We become a new creation

O God, restore our souls;
renew a right spirit within us

We pray with those we know in our church
and in your world
who suffer bodily pain and mental anguish

Receive now our silent petitions and questions:

Silent prayer

Amen

❉ ❉ ❉ ❉

ONE MORE ORDINARY DAY
Ninth Sunday in Ordinary Time

Give ear to our words,
O Rock and Redeemer,
whose glory
is chanted above the heavens
by the mouths of babes and infants

Pay attention to the sound of our voices,
for to you
we pray

We come this morning,
deep in the days of ordinary time,
sometimes embarrassed to call your name
and to say again
that ordinary life here in ordinary time
seems complicated and hard, and sometimes hurts;
confessing that we have
in the hurry and mess of living
forgotten to awaken with songs of gratefulness
to you on our lips

We come, God, confessing that in some moments,
we look upon the beloved faces in our lives,
across our dinner tables,
and fail to gasp thanksgivings to you
for the miracle of those faces and our love for them.
Shock us back into your presence
with the daily holy moments
that surround us.
Compel us to live
ordinary lives of extraordinary depth, for which
we were made

Even as you released Israel from her captors,
leading her with pillar of fire by night
and cloud by day,
we pray for release
from personal demons that would hold us captive,
from burdens within our community

that would keep us in exile,
and for all those imprisoned around your world.
We pray for your justice and your mercy,
flowing like flooded rivers

Hear us now, as we lift our
longings and thanksgivings
to you:

Prayers of intercession

Accept our prayers.
In your mercy, look with compassion upon us,
for you are gracious, O Lover of souls

AMEN

❋ ❋ ❋ ❋

BORN OF WATER AND SPIRIT
Tenth Sunday in Ordinary Time

God, your Spirit stirred over the face of the waters
and brought forth light and life.
We gather to worship your Child
brought forth from the waters of Mary's womb,
revealed as your own beloved Child in the waters of
the River Jordan and the Spirit's descent.
Hear now the prayers of your people,
your children born of water and spirit

We praise you
and give you thanks

for the church of Jesus Christ,
where two or three
or millions around this world
gather together in your name
and proclaim to this world
the good news—
that God is with us,
and this world
will be loved
into wholeness.
We thank you for your church, God,
where protests are made on behalf of the tired,
the battered, the hungry;
where ordinary lives and extraordinary kindnesses are
celebrated

We thank you for our directive
to do your work in this world,
for the call to see injustices righted.
We thank you for the mercy and forgiveness
we have found here,
the tears wiped away,
the hands held,
the gifts given,
and the children treasured and nurtured

For we were formed in your image,
and it is your face, God, that
we find among us here.
For we were called by your Child's voice,
and in this place it is Jesus' voice we hear.
We are here, God,
wet with baptismal waters

because we believe that you work
miracles from earthen vessels such as we are

Guide us as we go to the sick,
the grieving,
the lonely,
the hungry,
not with a stone but with comfort and bread

Deep in the midst of the miracle we call life,
we bring our petitions and thanksgivings to you:

Prayers of intercession

AMEN

❋ ❋ ❋ ❋

THE BLESSING OF
NOISY GREETINGS
Eleventh Sunday in Ordinary Time

O holy, amazing God
who so loved the world that
your Christ dwelt among us,
we come this morning
amazed still that you love us

We are full of gratitude, God, for the blessing
of noisy greetings between brothers and sisters in Christ.
For it is in the loving eyes of this community that we are
led to your presence.
It is in the forgiving eyes of our sisters and brothers
in Christ

that we learn to forgive ourselves
and we learn to believe in your forgiveness of us

We pray today for the oppressed in our nation,
our community,
our neighborhoods,
who know hunger and deprivation.
Give us eyes to see the economic violence
in our own nation and our own lives.
Reveal to us what it means to be our sisters'
and our brothers'
keepers.
Stand with us in giving strength as we respond

In the deep beauty of the earth,
we pray today for all who are ill.
In the warmth of ordinary time in summer,
there are those who know the cold reality of
being shut out of relationship,
finding only hard answers,
feeling powerless

Only you, God, know the innermost longings of our hearts,
and now silently we uncover them ourselves:

Silent prayer

We pray these things in the name of the Christ,
who, though no longer a babe,
is always being reborn,
moment by moment in the community
gathered here and around the world this morning

AMEN

❊ ❊ ❊ ❊

WE GATHER AS BROTHERS AND SISTERS

Twelfth Sunday in Ordinary Time

O God, our Refuge and our Strength,
we gather gratefully as brothers and sisters in Christ,
made in your image,
called to proclaim the good news

We come rejoicing
with loud songs of joy
for the beauty of the earth, the glory of the skies;
for the love, which from our birth, over and around us lies

And we come with sorrow,
wondering where refuge will be found
for the homeless,
for the poor whom Jesus named as blessed

Soften our hearts, God,
so we may clearly hear the stranger's knock
at our door

Give us tender hearts, O Holy One,
in this noisy world where horror and violence
threaten to become ordinary, accepted.
Give us tender hearts to stand firm against the
hardness of the world.
Flood us with courage
to take hold of this noisy, numb world and say "No!"
Flood us with courage
to risk the inevitable pain that comes with loving one
another

Soften our hearts, dear God,
to one another,
that in learning to bear one another's limits and aggravations,
we learn to pray for one another

O God, we are constant in our desire for you.
Silently we wait for you to receive and to fill our hearts
as we empty ourselves to you
with our silent prayers:

Silent prayer

We pray for the sick, the lonely, the grieving,
that your grace may bring comfort, the miracle of healing,
and company in the midst of sorrow

We remember and give thanks this morning
for the cloud of witnesses, strengthening us
to run with perseverance the race that is set before us

We pray to be aglow in the Spirit,
so that we may rejoice in hope,
remain patient in tribulation,
and be constant in prayer

AMEN

❊ ❊ ❊ ❊

COURAGE LIKE WATER
FROM THE ROCK
Thirteenth Sunday in Ordinary Time
Labor Day Sunday

O God,
you are so gracious and good.
Your bounty of love for us
would gather us
as a mother hen
gathers her young

In this world of plenty,
we try to live like the lily of the field
and the sparrow,
without fear of what we will eat next
and what we will put on next.
In this world of miracles you created for us,
we try to love fully,
sorting what is of significance in this life
from the unnecessary and the draining.
But there are moments, God,
when we loosely spend the breath of life
you have given us—
sometimes in fear of tomorrow,
in fear of what we will eat,
and in fear of the restriction of our own inabilities

God of creation,
hear our silent confessions and thanksgivings:

> *Silent prayer*

In your creation of this world
which is good,
we long, God, to know that we are good.
In this created world that you made beautiful,
we long to know that we, too, are a creation made beautiful.
Help us find reflected in us what
we see every day in your creation

Call forth from us
courage
which, like water from the rock,
will sustain us from the depths

We thank you [on this Labor Day weekend]
for the task of useful work.
Bless all who labor.
We pray for workers across this world,
unprotected in dangerous circumstances

We pray for the unseen workers,
those who lift and clean
and nurture the bodies and minds and the spirits
of those we love who are in hospitals and hospice care

Hear our prayers for the plight of workers
laboring without medical insurance, retirement

Receive our prayers for unemployed workers and their families,
that anxiety may be allayed
and fears relieved,
that justice and work will be restored to them

Still, O Holy One,
our restless hearts;
help us know the work you would have us do,
bringing our lives to fruitfulness

In your mercy,
bless those who grieve;
guide us in their comforting

In your mercy,
hear our prayers for the sick and heartsick

AMEN

❊ ❊ ❊ ❊

REMAKE US AGAIN
Fourteenth Sunday in Ordinary Time

O God, whose breath and word inspire
the heavens and the earth into being,
you shape us to your image
and command that we make no other image of you

Be close this morning;
re-form us again
as you formed us once
in our mothers' wombs,
that our flesh and spirit
may respond to you
as did Israel in its youth

Like the ones Jesus healed,
we come,
some of us longing to be remade again,
some of us grieving over choices made
and opportunities lost,
some of us heartsick
with a burden that will not let us go

Hear our prayers for those who know the
anguish of having a loved one in prison.
Hear our petitions for those of us
who know the misery and shame
of alcohol or food addictions.
Speak a word
to those whose limbs and hearts are deadened by depression
or whose lives have become unbearable from anxiety and dread

For our own church,
where our suffering is held and gently relieved,
we offer you
humble hearts
and thanksgiving
for our ancestors
who imagined a house of worship
and sacrificed and rejoiced and planned and built it

For the great-great-grandchildren of this church,
whose future and names and lives we cannot know
but can only provide for,
we ask for wisdom and insight and integrity
to create for them a possible future of worship and learning,
as those long ago had the foresight
to create what shelters us now

Even as we give you thanks for this community,
we know
that of those to whom much is given,
much will be required

Build of us a people with gentle hearts,
whose every beginning and every ending
is found in you

AMEN

❊ ❊ ❊ ❊

WHY DO THE JUST SUFFER
AND THE WICKED PROSPER?
Fifteenth Sunday in Ordinary Time

O God,
you knew us before we were knit together
in our mothers' wombs.
Upon you we were cast from our birth

Since our mothers bore us,
you have been our God.
Hear when we cry unto you;
be gracious unto us

As summer heat begins to give way,
we are amazed
that another summer has come and gone
and the vast beauty of fall and its harvest gifts
await us

Have mercy on us, God,
when we note time's swift passing
more often than we thank you
for each moment of its being

We come this morning
imploring you,
like the psalmist,
"Why do the just suffer
and the wicked prosper?"
Is it something that we,
your people, have committed against you?
Is it something we have done,
or is it something we have failed to do—
that the hungry have no food,
the impoverished have no shelter?

Have mercy on us;
touch to our lips a burning coal
as you did your servant Isaiah,
that we might have our missing-the-mark
forgiven.
Purify our hearts
until truth as you would speak it
abides within us

Give us, O God, a love worthy
of suffering with those who
search after righteousness

Give us a love courageous enough
to suffer with those who know
the wound of illness,

the marks of disease,
the fear of dying

And for those newborn, give us a love
worthy of all that is full of promise,
that they might know you as the source of their hope
and their life

Help us to know, O God,
in the midst of our own brief passage,
what is worth the effort of our energy,
what is worth the passing and the handing on
from one life to another

Accept our humble and silent
prayers to you now:

> *Silent prayer*

For those who grieve shall be comforted,
and those who hunger shall be fed

AMEN

❦ ❦ ❦ ❦

WE LONG FOR RELATIONSHIP
Sixteenth Sunday in Ordinary Time

O God, who first loved and whose persistent love endures,
hear the prayers of your people,
who gather to worship
astounded

by the love that
gathers us again and again
into community before you

You created it and named it good
and set the earth spinning,
making the tides ebb and flow.
Hear our prayers for our brothers and sisters
whose homes and lives have been forever changed
by natural disasters, violence, death

We dare to imagine, God,
a community of your people where the power of the Spirit
and the force of living water
can change human hearts,
washing clean the damage
we have made
against you,
against one another

We are eager, God,
to embody the relationship you hungered for
in creating humans for one another
and for relationship with you

We, too, are stubborn, God.
We persist in seeking your presence
as we form relationships one to another.
And more especially, God,
we long
to construct community and good
as powerful as the wind and water of your creation.
Show us the way

God,
we cannot comprehend the permanent separation
from our loved ones that death brings.
We especially do not understand the deaths of children
and of parents with children.
You alone are God,
and for your mercy we weep

For the people of this world
who face oppressive regimes and violence,
we ask for courage in the face of hopelessness

We remember those in our church family
who know pain this morning
as we remember those across your earth who suffer.
Be with us
as we take a cup of cool water to them
in your name

AMEN

✤ ✤ ✤ ✤

WE COME IMPERFECT, DISSATISFIED, AND HUNGRY
Seventeenth Sunday in Ordinary Time

O God of mercy,
we come into your presence,
captives of time and space,
captive to these bodies,
these minds and hearts and souls.

We come longing for release
into your creating
breath of life

We come imperfect, dissatisfied,
and hungry
to love you.
Accept our worship

We sense that all—
every creation and the breath of life
and its companion, death—
are miracles of your breath, God, among us.
Yet we doubt and wait,
hoping for something written on the wall,
hoping for certainty
beyond our
knowing

We come wishing we were better,
hoping the prodigal story is a true one for us personally,
finding it difficult to believe
your invitation to us is
constantly present,
spreading a table for us

God, we believe;
help our unbelief

For the breadth of your mercy,
we are forever daily grateful.
Steady us
to be widely merciful

with our sister and brother
when we experience frustration with one another—
offended by one another's differences,
possessive of our own gods

Rebuke us when we fail to forgive
even as we have been forgiven

Even greater than our frustrations, O Holy of Holies,
is our thankfulness
for acts of kindness that
make our hardened hearts
tender again

For the men, women, and children of this church
and the cloud of witnesses among us,
for your church throughout the world,
we give thanks
and pray for wisdom

Descend now
in the hands and faces and feet of this congregation,
that we might
comfort those who grieve.
Bind up the wounds of the sorrowful
and be present to those who suffer,
knowing severe limits in body and mind

AMEN

❧ ❧ ❧ ❧

WE WANT TO BE YOURS,
GOD, IN THE MIDST OF TIME
Eighteenth Sunday in Ordinary Time

Creating God, who set the earth on its foundations,
we come in the spinning of time
and the passing of seasons,
praising you,
longing to encompass all time
and span all space
as together we become the body of Christ

We remember as we pray this morning
the churches gathering throughout your world.
We remember our missionaries,
[list the names of your faith community's missionaries],
working to serve you in loyalty and justice in
[list where the missionaries are serving]
even as we try to do your work here at home.

Prayers of intercession

In this season of fall, we remember other fall seasons.
Some of us come with the joyful and clear voices of children;
some of us, with the steady comfortable voice
of the years of middle life; and
still others, with the voice of many years lived.
We long, God, to join those voices together
to be yours in the midst of our lives,
regardless of time or of our age.
For we are here so short a time;
like the grasses of the field,

we flourish and wither.
Help us to number our days,
that we might apply our hearts to wisdom

We would do your bidding, God,
as we grow;
as we come, as a church, to discern our future.
Grant us vision in these many days of ordinary time,
that the extraordinary be manifest
and compelling to us;
that we become part of your wisdom,
sorting out what is temporary
from what is real, lasting, life-giving

Help us beyond our immediate concerns, commitments,
and Little League games
to remember the movement of two thousand years of time
since Christ.
Help us commit acts of love that never fade away,
acts of love that are inconvenient.
Help us commit acts of love
that threaten the false security
we have been lulled into

We pray for ourselves
and for our church.
Guide us in the paths of righteousness for your sake

AMEN

❀ ❀ ❀ ❀

EMBRACE US IN OUR MOURNING
AND IN OUR FEARS, GOD
Nineteenth Sunday in Ordinary Time

Great, living God,
for all the families of this world,
we ask your abiding and steadfast love:
that father, mother, stepparent, sister, brother, child,
might be to one another
an ever-present help in time of need;
that we might know strength in time of sorrow,
encouragement and joy in daily relationships and work

God, be in our midst, in this family of God which
we call "church,"
that we might be known to one another
through the fruits of the Spirit—
patience, kindness, peacefulness

Heal us,
that we, like Israel,
might respond to you as in the days of our youth—
like a child,
transparent to your love

Turn us,
so that in our turning around,
we find a table prepared for us,
even in the midst of our enemies
of self-doubt, self-deceit

We long to know the lightness of your burden, God,
because often we do not understand
the yoke of ease your Child promised

Many of us come today
with a heaviness that won't give way.
Even in the magnificence of this life
and the beauty of the earth,
our hearts surely will break with sorrow.
Receive our sorrow

Abide with us in health and in illness
as we abide with one another.
Embrace us in our mourning and fears.
Strengthen us,
that we might
know your strength
and sustenance
in danger
and safety,
in laughter and in sorrow

Be with us, God.
Be our rest

AMEN

❋ ❋ ❋ ❋

BUILD IN US A HOUSE OF REST
Twentieth Sunday in Ordinary Time

O God
who seeks to build in us a house of rest,
be with us this morning in the solitude
of our hearts
and the communion of this community

Abide with us
as we attend to the falling of leaves,
watching the faithful turning of your creation earth
in its cycle of life,
birth,
fulfillment,
and death

We long to be as faithful
in our lives
as your creation is
in its turning to you

It is a troublesome thing to be made in your image
without your wisdom.
And so our hearts ache
and our spirits wither;
and we come to you again,
confessing things we have done,
things we have left undone

You know
that because of our missing the mark,
we create realities
based on what we do
or on who loves us.

And like the foolish one
who built a house on the sand,
we
are vulnerable and easily destroyed.
We are anxious and afraid
beneath the surface of things,
holding our lives together
by stories we thought or hoped
were real

Let Wisdom build herself a home
in which our hearts
can heal and be healed
from wounds,
heartaches of those we have sinned against,
and our pain from those who have broken our hearts

God, we will never understand illness and suffering;
and so, failing understanding,
we will bring our presence to bear
like the Marys at the foot of the cross

But you must bring the light unto our path
as we go,
or we will not carry your comfort in our visit.
For it is your peace that heals,
your rest that quiets our hearts

Blessed be you, O God,
and blessed be your name

    AMEN

    ❧ ❧ ❧ ❧

WE THIRST FOR YOU, GOD
Twenty-first Sunday in Ordinary Time

God,
we come to you
as we are:
some of us exultant, feeling fully the promise of life abundant;
some of us broken, wondering what happened to a vision or
a commitment
or even what happened to the self we used to know.
Some of us come this day feeling the sorrow of regret
for words spoken before we could inhale them
back into our mouths.
Some of us bring the particular grief of realizing
in hindsight that our time or energy or love has been misspent

Sorrowful or joyful,
regret-filled or full of hope,
we thirst for you, God.
For you we ache like a dry and weary land

Hear our silent longings and thanksgivings:

Silent prayer

Hear our prayers for this church,
that we might be for one another
a strength in uncertainty,
a counselor in perplexities,
a comfort in sorrow,
and companions in joy

We pray today for those who have died for liberty
in the past centuries
and this past year, in struggles against tyrannies around the world.
We ask to know this kind of courage,
that someone would lay down
their own life
for the lives of many

We are trying, God,
to bear witness to your love in this world.
We want those to whom love is a stranger
to find in this community generous friends.
Renew us, sustain us, fill us for this work

For the ill, we ask for miraculous healing.
For those of us who know anxiety and despair,
we petition you for relief and a restored future.
Knowing those who wait upon you
shall renew their strength.
They shall mount up with wings like eagles.
They shall run and not be weary.
They shall walk and not be faint

Let it be, God.
Let it be

AMEN

❀ ❀ ❀ ❀

HOW LONG, O GOD?
Twenty-second Sunday in Ordinary Time

God of love and wonder,
you clothe the lilies of the field
and fill this earth
with good things

We come to you
offering praise,
for you have done
wonderful things

We come to you, hearts full of joy,
magnifying your creation,
that new life is born and sustained
among us.
And
we come to you
in anguished whispers,
our voices tight with tears,
for the unspeakable agony of loss we know in this life

Hear our praise,
accept our anguish,
for you alone are God.
For you, we ache and thirst
like a dry and weary land

We wonder, God,
that you receive
the thousands of souls of hungry children
who starve to death daily.

We wonder that it would happen
in a world where God is good—
and we realize you must wonder that it happens
in a world you created good—
with food enough for all.
How you must mourn over the choices we make
and the effects they have
on your children throughout the world!

We confess we have sinned.
We have failed to love you with our whole heart.
We have built our lives upon securities which are
vulnerable to rust and moths and thieves.
We feel the sand foundation we built on
beginning
to wash away,
out from under us

Forgive us
and hear our silent longings,
confessions, and thanksgivings
as we bring them to you:

   Silent prayer

We pray for our world,
that we might know peace.
How long, O God,
how long
must we endure
the agony of
this madness called "warring"?

Make us peace-full then
in the name of your Child of peace

AMEN

❉ ❉ ❉ ❉

ACCEPT THE GIFTS WE BRING
Twenty-third Sunday in Ordinary Time
Thanksgiving Sunday

O Wondrous One,
whose hands wrought
life and breath into
this planet that sustains all life,
we come at this time of harvest,
our hands burdened
with the fruits of your fields,
knowing your goodness,
your abundant love,
through
the infinite gifts of
your earth

Accept the gifts we bring;
look graciously on us.
Generously accept what we return to you today

We desire such courage and determination
as our ancestors possessed
to cross an expanse of ocean,
leaving all of home behind,

in exchange for the stony heart of wilderness
out of love for you

For the Native Americans,
who in mercy and tenderheartedness
assisted them,
we give you thanks
even as we confess our hubris
and our sin
in exploiting them and taking for ourselves
the land, the freedom, the resources
that were their birthright

For a country
marvelous and yet deeply imperfect,
help us in our striving for liberty and justice
for all.
Come to our aid as we work to
repair our oppressive behaviors against one another.
For the possibility of such repair,
we give you thanks

We ask that you multiply our gifts
until, like the little boy's fishes and loaves,
they feed multitudes

We hope to know, God,
what that little boy knew:
that the fertile soil of miracles
is sharing

Because out of nothing came being,
out of obscurity came light,
out of dust came life;

because in the midst of meaninglessness,
you call us to meaning;
in the midst of divisiveness,
you call us to community;
out of brokenness,
you call us to wholeness;
we praise you, God,
for your wondrous gifts

AMEN

❊ ❊ ❊ ❊

SHARING OUR BOUNTIFUL TABLES
Twenty-fourth Sunday in Ordinary Time

God,
you smote the rock so that water gushed out,
and spread a table of manna,
the grain of heaven,
in the midst of the wilderness.
Hear our prayers

As we gather amidst
a bountiful harvest,
hear our grateful praise for the table
your Child spreads for us

Walk beside us,
steadying us
as we learn to share our bountiful tables
until the hungry are fed.
Chasten us

until we accept your bountiful gifts,
not as blessings gratefully received
but as the loaves and fishes
from which you would have us feed the world

You call us to doing justice
and loving kindness.
You sent a beloved Child of justice,
who overturned the tables of moneychangers.
You sent a beloved Child of kindness,
who broke bread with the unloved
and unlovable.
We hope, God,
that your
kind
and just Child
would be comfortable at our tables
this Sunday noon

Scrape the scales from our eyes
until, like Paul on the Damascus road,
we see anew
and receive courage and vision
to overturn unjust tables
and break bread mercifully
with those to whom the world is not merciful

We pray for reconciliation
of your church throughout the world.
We pray for missionaries
across our country and the world,
who work to spread Christ's table
among those who suffer injustice

We remember church leaders
in our church
and in the world,
whose responsibilities and burdens
can be met only with your help
and ours,
O God

Endure with us.
Strengthen us.
Abide in us

AMEN

❊ ❊ ❊ ❊

THANK YOU FOR
THE JOSEPH STORY
Twenty-fifth Sunday in Ordinary Time

To you, O Holy One who first loved,
we bring our hands and hearts
this Sabbath morning.
We have come, God,
to praise you in the assembly,
to re-create the body of Christ.
We have come because
we become together
what we are not singularly.
Hear our grateful hymns as
we become whole, joining one another
in prayer and praise

We praise you for each child
in our church community,
for the blessing and teaching and challenge
they bring to us.
We thank you for the Joseph story.
We pray that we learn to dream dreams
like Joseph
and like children do—
dreams that have not been clipped by living and adulthood,
dreams that are unpopular when heard,
dangerous dreams
like the ones Joseph described.
Surely your dramatic creation and its setting sun
remind us to dream new ways of being and doing in this world
that none has imagined before

We thank you for families,
for Jacob and Rachel's love of one another
and the blessings of marriage in our midst.
We thank you for a father's beloved gift
of a robe to a son.
We pray especially today for fathers and mothers who love
unconditionally,
boldly displaying it to the world

Wake us to the many-colored robes of love
each of us has to bestow on one another.
Like Dinah and Joseph's other, unnamed sisters,
let our hands and hearts
spin and weave and toil
to provide garments of love
in abundance

We thank you for Reuben's
torn feelings
between jealousy and loyalty and love.
We are grateful, God, to see ourselves in the
human story of the Bible.
Most especially, we are grateful that
such torn feelings are not the last word,
and we pray for
the reconciliation of brothers,
sisters, families,
communities, and nations

We pray for those in our community who face illness,
who feel the vulnerability of life's fabric unraveling.
Comfort them, O God
knit up the hidden wounds of despair

AMEN

❧ ❧ ❧ ❧

FORGIVE US FOR OUR HURRIEDNESS AND IMPATIENCE
Twenty-sixth Sunday in Ordinary Time

God, who made the heavens
and whose love is everlasting,
we come into your presence
with thanksgiving and singing,
and brokenness and sorrow,
grateful for your presence

We come encouraged by what we have learned
and troubled by what we have not known,
hungry for you, Wise and Forgiving One

Forgive us for our hurriedness and impatience,
especially when we hurry our children
and when we impatiently leave no sacred space in our lives
for the Spirit to move

Forgive us when we act first
and pray for guidance second

Forgive us when our clay feet drag slowly against
injustice and the urgency of your gospel

As Mary recognized human need
at the wedding feast in Cana
and made it known to her child,
let us be moved by the needs of your people.
As the woman celebrates when the lost coin has been found,
surely you rejoice in our compassion for one another

In the peace and beauty of this sanctuary,
we remember lives that continue to bear witness
to the suffering and unspeakable human costs of war.
As we remember [this Memorial Day] those who died
and those who survived the wars in our lifetimes,
let us rededicate ourselves
to knowing your justice and your mercy, O God.
We do not yet know
how to be peace
in your world

Our heads are bowed in reverence this morning, God,
for the miracle of loving one another,
of being loved;
bowed in gratitude
for every intercessory prayer and word of kindness

Every loving act
for one another and for strangers
participates in your body, God.
For it is in caring for one another that
we come to taste your love, which informs all our loves

Help us to number our days,
that we will live our lives not in fear of our death
but that we will face our death
knowing we have lived
and that we lived in you

Let our hands and feet
seek out the sick and the needy,
even as our prayers have sought you

Hear our silent longings and thanksgivings:

Silent prayer

AMEN

❀ ❀ ❀ ❀

OUR PETITION IS FOR AN UNDERSTANDING HEART, FOR WISDOM

Twenty-seventh Sunday in Ordinary Time

O God of life and its companion, death,
we gather as your people,
knowing that a thousand years—
even ten times a thousand—
is not sufficient
to offer thankful praise
for this miracle,
the breath of life

With Solomon, we
bring ourselves before you,
and our petition is
for an understanding heart,
for wisdom

We come
feeling that we,
our talent, our treasure
are no more than a widow's mite.
Give us sight
when we
are blind to our wealth of talent.
Forgive us
when we bury our time and talent;
truly we long to give them to you.
For in you our hearts trust,
and in you our weary minds find courage and rest

For those who trust in God
will understand,
and we will hear your voice calling to us
that the winter is past,
the rain is over and gone,
and the time of singing has come.

Let it be, God.
Let it be

AMEN

❈ ❈ ❈ ❈

UNDERSTANDING THE INCOMPREHENSIBLE
Twenty-eighth Sunday in Ordinary Time

To you we lift our souls,
for you have been our dwelling place in all generations;
before the mountains were brought forth
or earth received its frame,
from everlasting to everlasting,
you are God

We gather before you this morning,
as every morning,
in a tangle of human relationship,
sisters and brothers in Christ,
whose love for one another
helps us to understand the incomprehensible—
your love for us—
and whose challenge to us sends us back again and again
to renew that tangle of loves

with all our
heart, mind, soul, and strength

We come perhaps most grateful of all
for this human community and
its forgiveness of us and its challenges
to us;
for it is through being forgiven
and challenged
that we learn to forgive
and to grow

As autumn moves toward winter,
we discover a homesickness,
a longing to see the warmth of the beloved faces
we are separated from, either through life
or through death.
We pray, God, for those people who are absent,
whom we carry in our hearts.
We bring you our hope for reunion

O Love!
That we might have your love and your courage
to shake the foundations of this world
until we can finally say to the one who called us, no longer
servants
but friends:
"Yes, we have fed the hungry.
Yes, we have clothed the naked.
Yes, we have housed the homeless."

Make us wise, God.
Call out to us,

like the widow at the judge's feet,
until we say yes to your creation
and to loving justice, doing mercy,
and walking humbly with you

Hear now our silent prayers:

Silent prayer

AMEN

❊ ❊ ❊ ❊

WE BLESS YOUR NAME
Twenty-ninth Sunday in Ordinary Time

O God, open our lips
and our mouths must speak your praise

You love us
even as we love our children.
We praise you for a love that comes to us
in many forms:
in the birth of a child,
in the touch of a friend in the midst of grief and hardship,
in the passion and commitment of a wife or husband,
in the courage of one fighting for justice

For your love informs all our loves
and comes to us in faces and hands
that we can see
and which make you known.
Your love reveals our belonging to you
in covenant

and in community.
We bless your name

Bless us
in right relationship to one another,
that we might hold each other gently,
calling forth in one another
the gifts that you have given
and the treasure you have hidden within each of us

We pray for a world that is turned too inward
and confess our own self-consciousness.
We have tied our lives down too much
in the work-and-spend cycle of possessions;
sowing nothing but the wind;
and reaping, we fear, a whirlwind
of human suffering—
a whirlwind wrapped in rootlessness
and inattention to the basic care
of our neighborhoods and of our world

We want to follow the Proverbs' instruction:
"at the cost of all you have, get understanding"

O Holy One,
if we cannot understand the tragedy of sudden death,
or the suffering of children,
or the gnawing and constant pains of poverty,
or the agony of suffering physical abuse,
then grant to us at least the hands to welcome
those who suffer so,
eyes to weep with them,
and feet to stand steadfast by them

If we cannot grasp with our minds,
let us seek with our hearts,
that failing in understanding,
we do not fail in courage and faith as well

AMEN

❦ ❦ ❦ ❦

scripture index